dingen	[dinguh]
dingen	[dinguhn]
もの	[monoh]
things	[things]
choses	[shoazuh]
Dinge	[deenguh]
cosas	[koasas]
cose	[koaze]
أشياء	[esheea]
şeyler	[sheler]

Nederlands	[nayduhlands]
Frysk	[freesk]
にほんご	[neehongoh]
English	[inglish]
Français	[franse]
Deutsch	[doitsh]
Español	[espanyol]
Italiano	[eetaleeahno]
اللغة العربية	[al ahrabeeya]
Türkçe	[tewrktshuh]

[outsprahk]   uitspraak

[ewtsprahk]   utspraak

[hatsoo-on]   はつおん

[pronunshayshuhn]   pronunciation

[proanonseeashon]   prononciation

[ousspraghuh]   Aussprache

[proanunthyathyon]   pronunciación

[pronoontsha]   pronunzia

[annotk]   النطق

[suhleneesh]   söyleniş

auto	[outoa]
auto	[oatoa]
トラック	[tuhrak]
car	[kar]
voiture	[vooahtewre]
Auto	[outoa]
coche	[kotshe]
macchina	[makkeena]
سيارة	[sayara]
araba	[arraba]

kitap	[keetap]
boek	[book]
boek	[book]
ほん	[hon]
book	[book]
livre	[leevruh]
Buch	[boogh]
libro	[leebro]
libro	[leebro]
كتاب	[keetehb]

   [meestara]

cetvel   [dzhetwel]

liniaal   [leeneeahl]

liniaal   [leeneeahl]

ものさし   [monosashee]

ruler   [rooluh]

règle   [regl]

Lineal   [leenayahl]

regla   [regla]

riga   [reega]

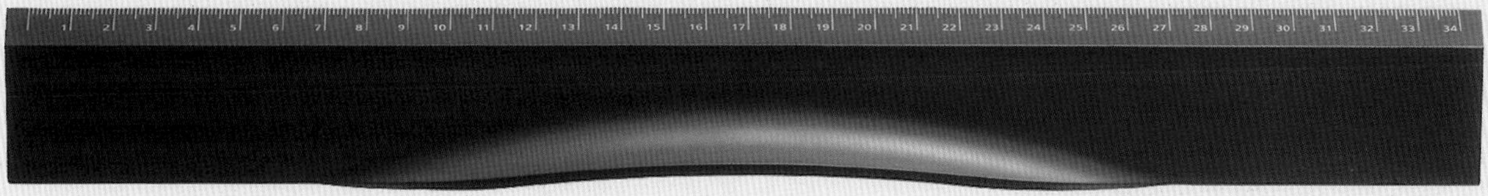
1 2 3 4 5 6 7 8 9 10 11 12 13 14 15 16 17 18 19 20 21 22 23 24 25 26 27 28 29 30 31 32 33 34

bottiglia	[botteelya]
قنينة	[keeneena]
şişe	[sheeshe]
fles	[fles]
flesse	[flessuh]
びん	[been]
bottle	[botl]
bouteille	[booteiy]
Flasche	[flashuh]
botella	[botelya]

reloj [raylogh]

orologio [orolodzho]

ساعة حائط [seahto ha-it]

saat [saht]

klok [klok]

klok [klok]

とけい [tokyay]

clock [klok]

horloge [orlozh]

Uhr [oor]

Zahnbürste	[tsahnbewrstuh]
cepillo de dientes	[thaypeelyo day dientes]
spazzolino da denti	[spatsoleeno da dentee]
فرشاة أسنان	[foorshet esnehn]
diş fırçası	[deesh fuhrtshasuh]
tandenborstel	[tanduhborstuhl]
toskboarstel	[toskbo-ahsl]
はブラシ	[hahberashee]
toothbrush	[toothbrush]
brosse à dents	[bros a dang]

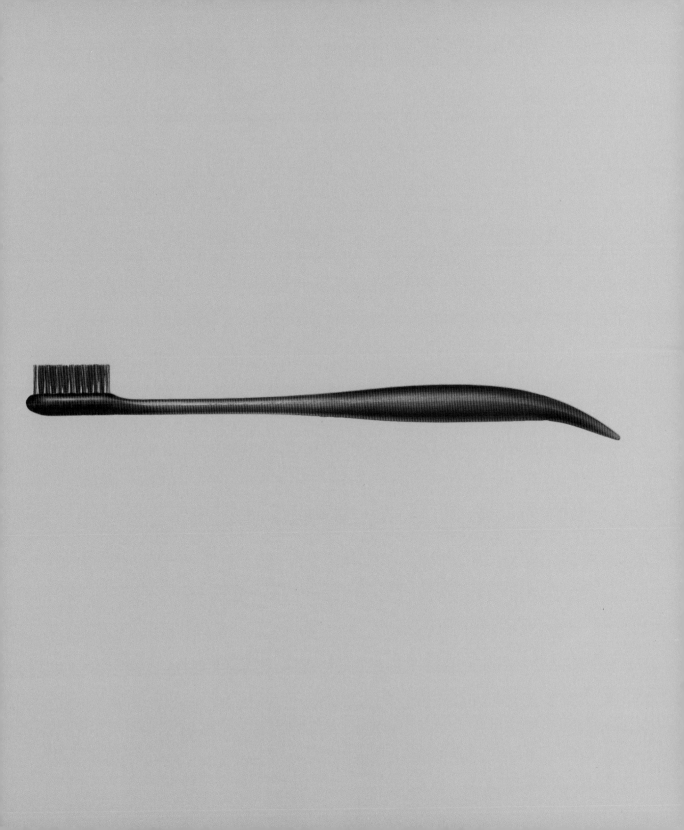

baladeur   [baladuah]

Walkman   [wolkman]

walkman   [wahlkmahn]

walkman   [wokmen]

مدياع نقال   [meedeeah nuhkuhl]

walkman   [walkmen]

walkman   [wokman]

walkman   [wokman]

ウォークマン   [wohkman]

walkman   [wohkmuhn]

coat stand	[koat stend]
portemanteau	[portmantoa]
Kleiderständer	[klaiduhrstenduhr]
perchero	[pertshayro]
attaccapanni	[attakkapannee]
مشجب	[meeshzheb]
askılık	[askuhluhk]
kapstok	[kapstok]
kapstôk	[kapstok]
コートかけ	[koatohkakke]

ゆうびんばこ [yoobeenbakkoh]

postbox [poastboks]

boîte aux lettres [booaht oa letruh]

Briefkasten [breefkastuhn]

buzón [boothon]

buca da lettere [bookah da lettuhruh]

صندوق البريد [sondoog al berreed]

posta kutusu [postah kootoosoo]

brievenbus [breevuhbus]

brievebus [breeahfuhbus]

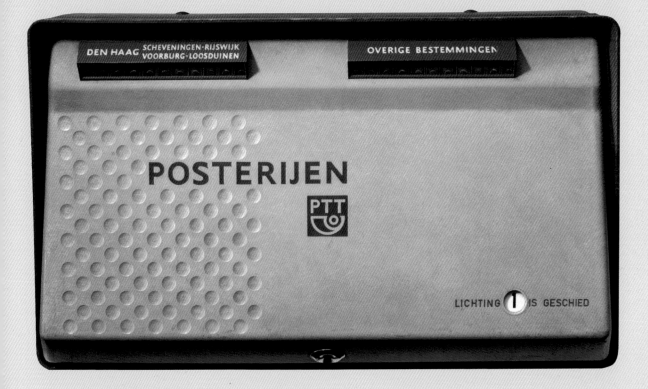

seage	[sayghuh]
のこぎり	[nokkohgiree]
saw	[so]
scie	[see]
Säge	[sayghuh]
sierra	[seeyerra]
sega	[saygah]
منشار	[meenshahr]
testere	[testere]
zaag	[zahgh]

mok	[mok]
mok	[mok]
コップ	[koppoo]
mug	[mug]
gobelet	[goable]
Becher	[beghuhr]
tazón	[tathon]
boccale	[bokkaluh]
كوب	[koob]
büyük fincan	[bewyewk feendzhan]

dikiş makinesi	[dee**kiesh** makeenessee]
naaimachine	[**nai**masheenuh]
naaimasine	[**nai**masheenuh]
ミシン	[**mee**sheen]
sewing machine	[**soa**wing muhsheen]
machine à coudre	[masheen a **koodr**]
Nähmaschine	[**nayh**masheenuh]
máquina de coser	[**ma**keena day koa**ser**]
macchina da cucire	[**mak**keena da koo**tshee**ruh]
اَلة الخياطة	[**ehl**let al ghey**a**ta]

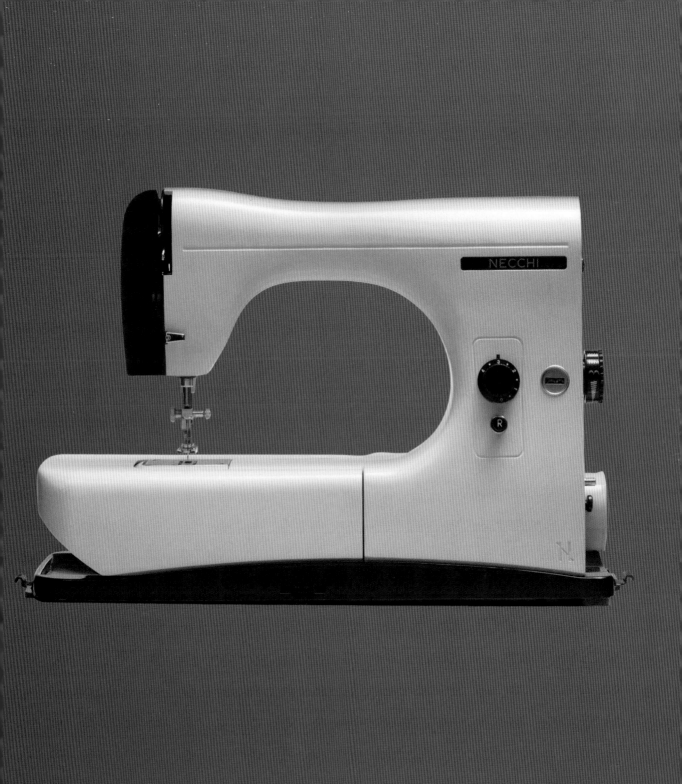

كأس	[ke-uhs]
bardak	[bardak]
glas	[ghlas]
glês	[gle-ahs]
グラス	[guhrasoo]
glass	[glahs]
verre	[ver]
Glas	[glahs]
copa	[kohpa]
bicchiere	[beekeeayruh]

aspirapolvere	[aspeerapolvuhruh]
مكنسة كهربائية	[meeknuhsuh kharabaheey
elektrik süpürgesi	[elektreek sewpewrgesee]
stofzuiger	[stofsoughuhr]
stofsûger	[stofsooghuhr]
そうじき	[zohdzheekee]
vacuum cleaner	[vekyoouhm kleenuh]
aspirateur	[aspeerateuh]
Staubsauger	[shtoubsouguh]
aspiradora	[aspeeradora]

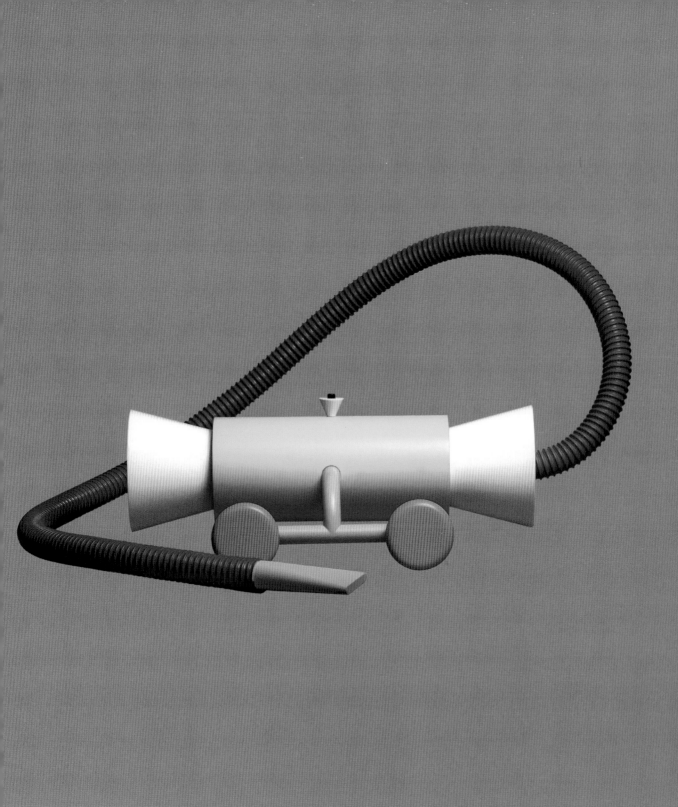

gafas	[gaf fas]
occhiali	[okkeealee]
نظارات	[naddarat]
gözlük	[guhzlewk]
bril	[bril]
bril	[bril]
めがね	[maygane]
spectacles	[spektukls]
lunettes	[lewnet]
Brille	[breeluh]

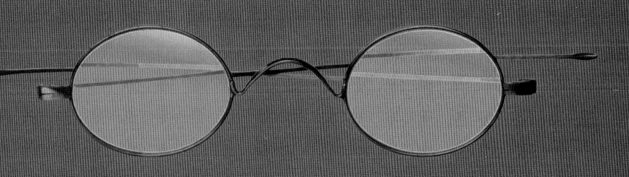

Wasserhahn	[wassuhrhahn]
grifo	[greefo]
rubinetto	[roobeenetto]
صنبور	[sanboor]
musluk	[mooslook]
kraan	[krahn]
kraan	[krahn]
じゃぐち	[dzhagoodzee]
tap	[tep]
robinet	[robbeene]

radio	[radyoa]
Radio	[rahdeeyoa]
radio	[radyo]
radio	[radeeo]
المذياع	[al meedee-ehr]
radyo	[radyoa]
radio	[rahdeeoa]
radio	[rahdeeoa]
ラジオ	[rahdyo]
radio	[raydeeoa]

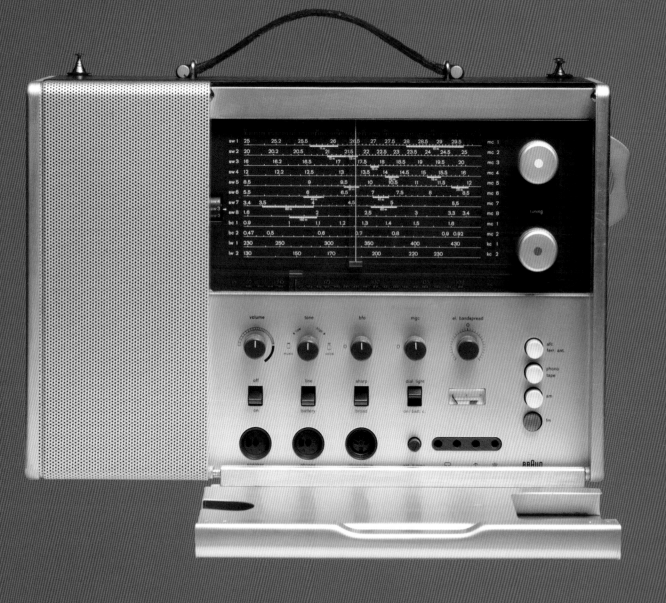

watch	[**wotsh**]
montre	[**montr**]
Uhr	[**oor**]
reloj de pulsera	[ray**logh** day pool**sayra**]
orologio	[oro**lo**dzho]
ساعة يد	[**sa**-aht yet]
kol saati	[**kol** satee]
horloge	[hor**loa**zhuh]
horloazje	[hor**loa**zhuh]
うでどけい	[ooded**do**kay]

gloeilampe	[glooilampuh]
でんきゅう	[denkeeoo]
light bulb	[lait bulb]
ampoule	[ampool]
Glühbirne	[glewbeernuh]
bombilla	[bombeelya]
lampadina	[lampadeena]
مصباح كهربائي	[meesbah kahrabeh-ee]
ampul	[ampool]
gloeilamp	[khlooilamp]

gloeilampe	[glooilampuh]
でんきゅう	[denkeeoo]
light bulb	[lait bulb]
ampoule	[ampool]
Glühbirne	[glewbeernuh]
bombilla	[bombeelya]
lampadina	[lampadeena]
مصباح كهربائي	[meesbah kahrabeh-ee]
ampul	[ampool]
gloeilamp	[khlooilamp]

つくえ [tskooe]

desk [desk]

bureau [bewroa]

Schreibtisch [shraibteesh]

escritorio [ayskreetorryo]

scrivania [skreevaneea]

مكتب [mekteb]

yazma masası [yazma massasuh]

bureau [bewroa]

buro [buhroa]

fototoestel	[foatoatoostel]
fototastel	[foatoatastel]
カメラ	[kamayra]
camera	[kemuhruh]
appareil photo	[appareiy foatoa]
Kamera	[kamuhra]
cámara	[kamara]
macchina fotografica	[makkeena fotografeeka]
آلة التصوير	[ahlatoo tassooeer]
fotoğraf makinesi	[fotohraf makeenessee]

kalem	[kalem]
pen	[pen]
pin	[pin]
ボールペン	[boo-ohroopen]
pen	[pen]
stylo bille	[steelo beel]
Stift	[steeft]
bolígrafo	[bolleegrafo]
penna	[penna]
قلم	[khuhluhm]

لوحة [laooha]

tablo [tabloa]

schilderij [sghilderai]

skilderij [skilduhrai]

え [ay]

painting [paynting]

tableau [tabloa]

Gemälde [gemaylduh]

cuadro [kooadro]

quadro [kwadro]

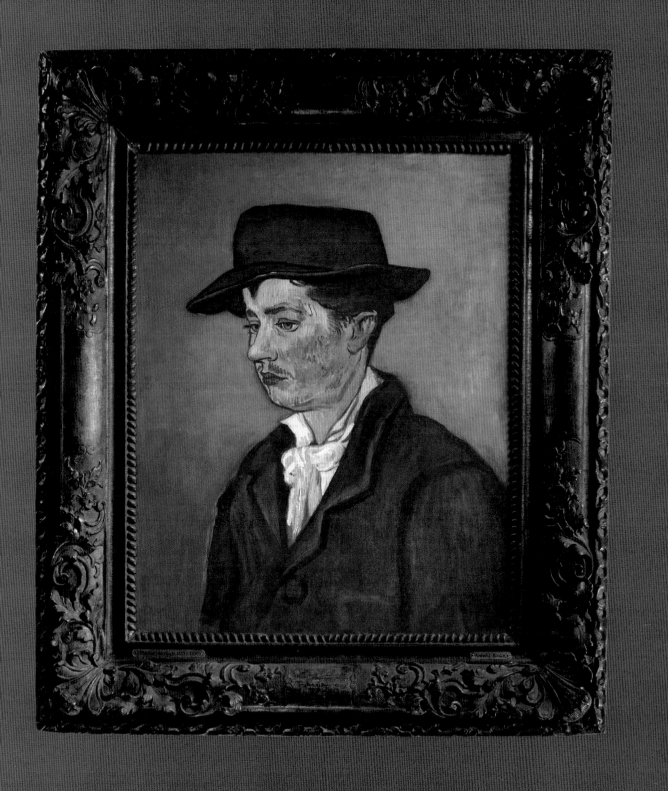

vaso	[vaso]
زهرية	[ze-hreea]
vazo	[wazo]
vaas	[vahs]
faas	[vahs]
かびん	[kahbeen]
vase	[vahs]
vase	[vahz]
Vase	[vahsuh]
florero	[florerro]

carretilla	[karre**teel**ya]
carriola	[karree**o**la]
عربة يد	[**ar**rabad yed]
el arabası	[**el** arabasuh]
kruiwagen	[**krou**wahghuh]
kroade	[**kroa**-ahde]
ておしぐるま	[ta**yo**sheegoorooma]
wheelbarrow	[**weel**berroa]
brouette	[broo**et**]
Schubkarre	[**shoop**karruh]

Pfeife	[pfaifuh]
pipa	[peepa]
pipa	[peepa]
غليون	[laleeoon]
pipo	[peepoh]
pijp	[paip]
piip	[peep]
パイプ	[paipoo]
pipe	[paip]
pipe	[peep]

CD	[sayday]
CD	[tsayday]
cd	[thayday]
CD	[tsheedee]
اسطوانة رقمية	[oostooahna rakmeea]
CD	[dzhede]
cd	[sayday]
cd	[sayday]
シーディー	[sheedee]
CD	[seedee]

paperclip	[**pay**puhklip]
trombone	[trom**bon**uh]
Büroklammer	[bew**roa**klammuhr]
sujetapapeles	[soo**ghe**tapa**pel**les]
clip	[**kleep**]
مشبك ورق	[**meesh**buhk aoo**rahk**]
kâğıt mandalı	[kya**huht** mandalluh]
paperclip	[**pay**puhklip]
klammerke	[**klam**muhrkuh]
クリップ	[**krip**poo]

じてんしゃ [dzhee**ten**sha]

bicycle [**bai**suhkl]

vélo [vay**loa**]

Fahrrad [**fahr**raht]

bicicleta [beethee**clay**ta]

bicicletta [beetshee**klet**ta]

دراجة [tar**ra**zha]

bisiklet [beesee**klet**]

fiets [**feets**]

fyts [**feets**]

rekkenmasine [**rekn**masheenuh]

けいさんき [kay**sang**kee]

calculator [**kel**kyuhlaytuh]

calculette [kalku**let**]

Taschenrechner [**ta**shenreghnur]

calculadora [kalkoola**do**ra]

calcolatrice [kalkola**tree**tshuh]

اَلة حاسبة [**e**luh **ha**seeba]

hesap makinesi [he**sap** makeenesee]

rekenmachine [**ray**kuhnmasheenuh]

kam	[kam]
kaam	[kahm]
くし	[kooshee]
comb	[koam]
peigne	[penyuh]
Kamm	[kam]
peine	[paynay]
pettine	[petteene]
مشط	[meesht]
tarak	[tarrak]

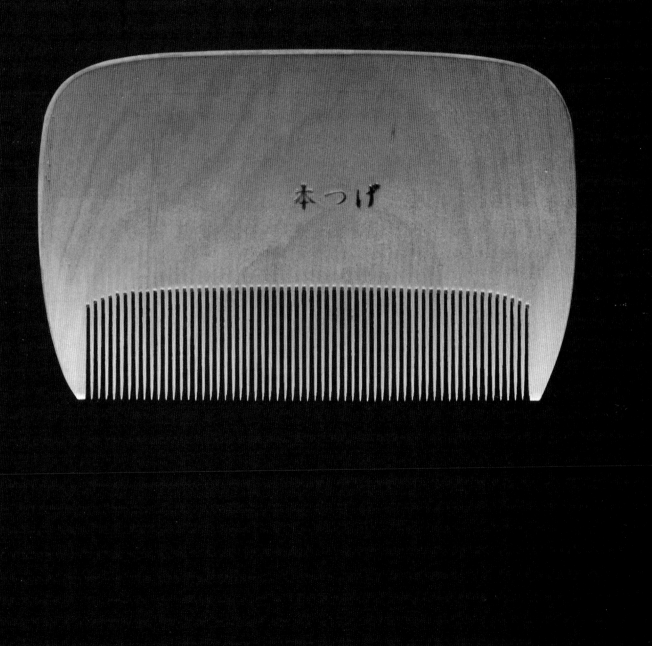

çamaşır leğeni	[tshamma**syuhr** layhenee]
teil	[tail]
tobke	[**top**kuh]
おけ	[oke]
tub	[tub]
cuvette	[kewh**vet**]
Kübel	[**kew**buhl]
barreña	[bar**ren**ya]
vasca	[**vas**ka]
وعاء	[ooiah-uh]

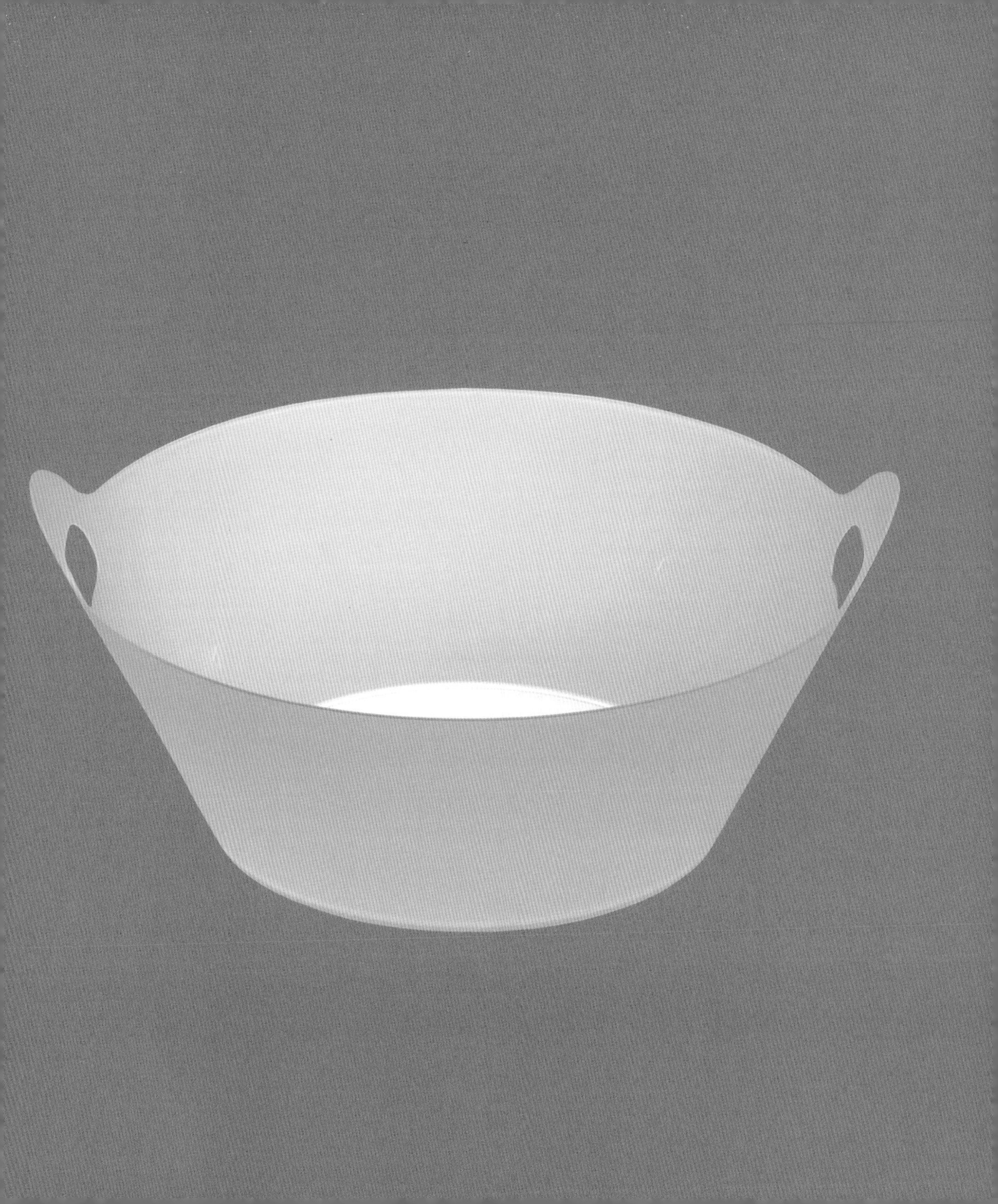

كرسي [koorsee]

sandalye [sandalye]

stoel [stool]

stoel [stoo-ahl]

いす [eezoo]

chair [tsheuh]

chaise [shez]

Stuhl [shtool]

silla [seelya]

sedia [saydeea]

ferro da stiro	[ferro da steero]
مكواة	[meekooeht]
ütü	[ewtew]
strijkbout	[straikbout]
strykizer	[streekeezuh]
アイロン	[aion]
iron	[aiuhn]
fer à repasser	[fer a repassay]
Bügeleisen	[bewguhlaisuhn]
plancha	[plantsha]

tijeras	[tee**ghay**ras]
forbici	[**for**beetshee]
مقص	[mee**kas**]
makas	[ma**kas**]
schaar	[sghahr]
skjirre	[sky**ir**ruh]
はさみ	[**ha**samee]
scissors	[**siz**uhs]
ciseaux	[see**soa**]
Schere	[**shay**ruh]

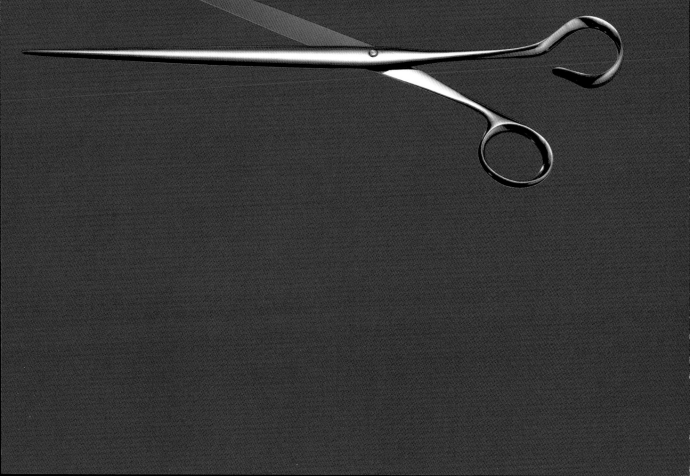

Tasse und Untertasse [tassuh oont oontuhrtassu

taza y platillo [tasa ee plateelyo]

tazza con piattino [tadzah kon peeatteeno]

فنجان وصحنه [feenzhen ooaseghnuh]

fincan ve tabağı [feendzhan we tabahuh]

kop en schotel [kop en sghoatuhl]

kop-en-pantsje [kop en pontshuh]

さらずきのちゃわん [sarazookee noh tshawan]

cup and saucer [kup end sosuh]

tasse et soucoupe [tas ay sookoop]

robe [robuh]

Kleid [klaid]

vestido [besteedo]

gonna [gonna]

فستان [foostehn]

elbise [elbeese]

jurk [yurk]

jurk [yurk]

ドレス [duhres]

dress [dres]

walking stick	[wohking stik]
canne	[kann]
Spazierstock	[shpatseershtok]
bastón	[baston]
bastone	[bastonuh]
عكاز	[oakehz]
baston	[baston]
wandelstok	[wanduhlstok]
kuierstôk	[kouerstok]
つえ	[tsooe]

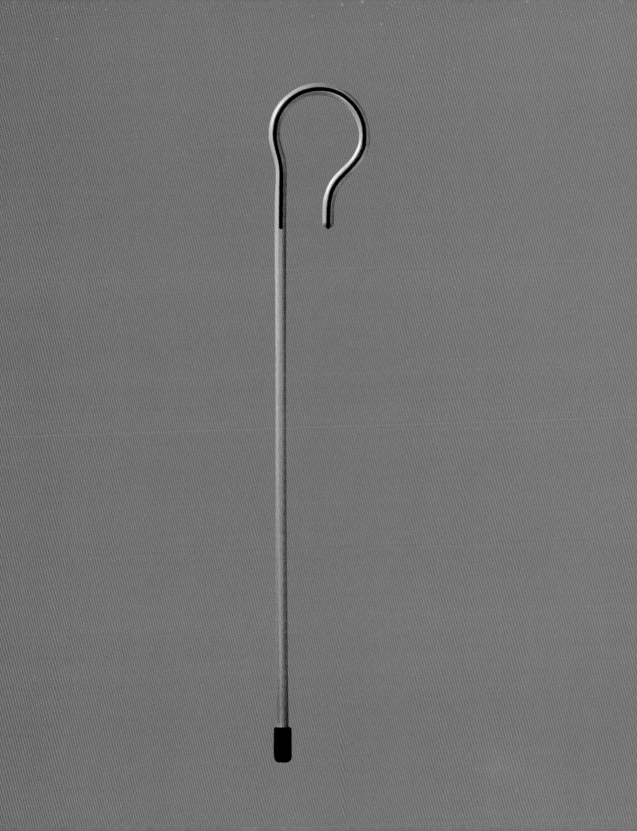

テーブル	[tayberoo]
table	[taybl]
table	[tabl]
Tisch	[teesh]
mesa	[messa]
tavola	[tavola]
مائدة	[me-eeda]
masa	[massa]
tafel	[tahfuhl]
tafel	[tahfuhl]

foarke	[furkuh]
フォーク	[fohk]
fork	[fok]
fourchette	[foorshet]
Gabel	[gahbuhl]
tenedor	[taynaydor]
forchetta	[forketta]
شوكة	[shooka]
çatal	[tshatal]
vork	[vork]

kan	[kan]
kanne	[konnuh]
みずさし	[meezoosashee]
jug	[dzhug]
pichet	[peeshe]
Kanne	[kannuh]
jarra	[gharra]
brocca	[brokka]
إبريق	[eebreeuhk]
testi	[testee]

dalgıç gözlüğü	[dal**guhtsh** guhzlehhew]
duikbril	[**douk**bril]
dûkbril	[**dook**bril]
ゴーグル	[**gog**geroo]
goggles	[**gogls**]
lunettes de plongée	[lew**net** de plon**zhay**]
Taucherbrille	[**tou**ghuhrbreeluh]
gafas de bucear	[**gaf**fas day boothe**ar**]
maschera subacquea	[**mas**kera sooba**kooa**]
نظارات الغطس	[nad**da**rat al rats]

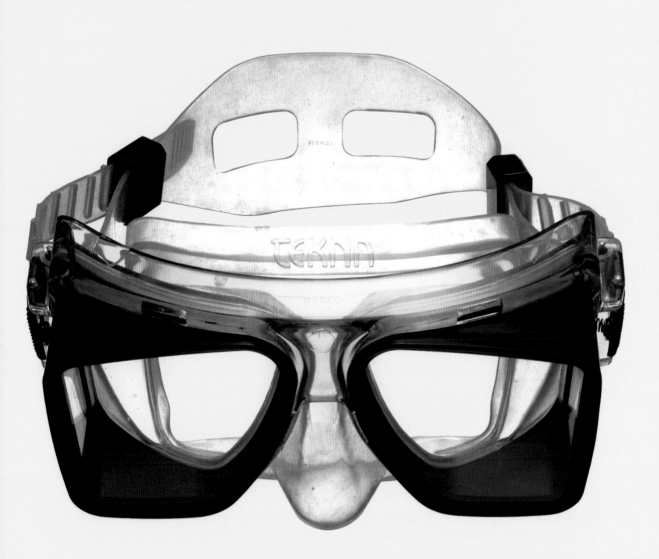

مـطرقة [meetrakka]

çekiç [tshekeetsh]

hamer [hahmuh]

hammer [hamr]

ハンマ [hamma]

hammer [hemuhr]

marteau [martoa]

Hammer [hammuh]

martillo [marteelyo]

martello [martello]

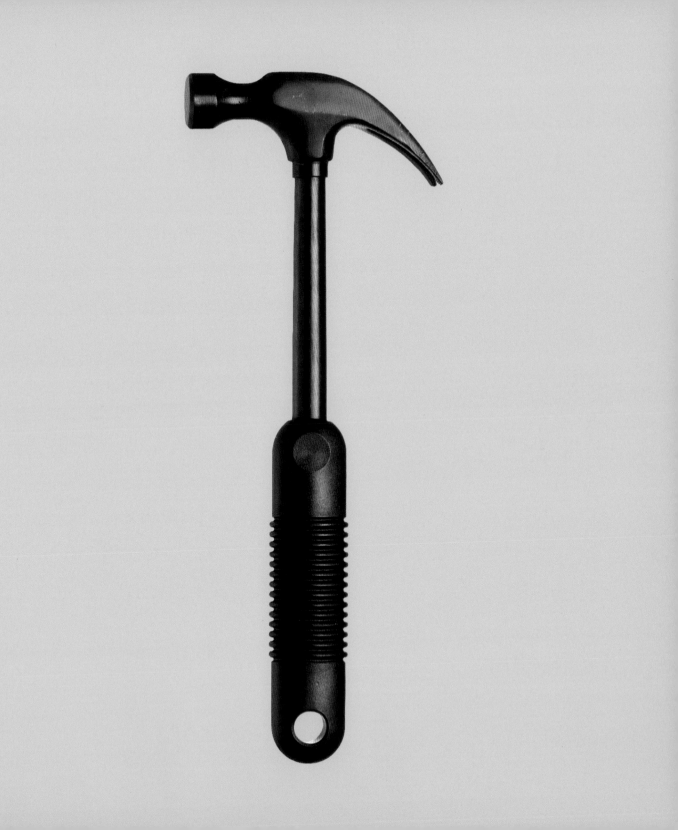

televisore	[taylayvee**so**ruh]
تلفاز	[teel**fehz**]
televizyon	[telewee**zhon**]
televisie	[tayluh**vee**zee]
televyzje	[tilluh**veez**hyuh]
テレビ	[**tay**rebee]
television set	[teluh**vizh**uhn set]
télévision	[taylayvee**zhon**]
Fernseher	[**fern**sayhuhr]
televisor	[taylayvi**sor**]

patinete	[pati**net**tay]
monopattino	[monopat**tee**no]
دراجة	[dah**rah**dzha]
trotinet	[trotee**net**]
step	[**step**]
autopet	[**ou**toapet]
かたあしスクーター	[kata-**ash**ee**skoo**ta]
scooter	[**skoo**tuh]
trottinette	[trottee**net**]
Roller	[rol**luhr**]

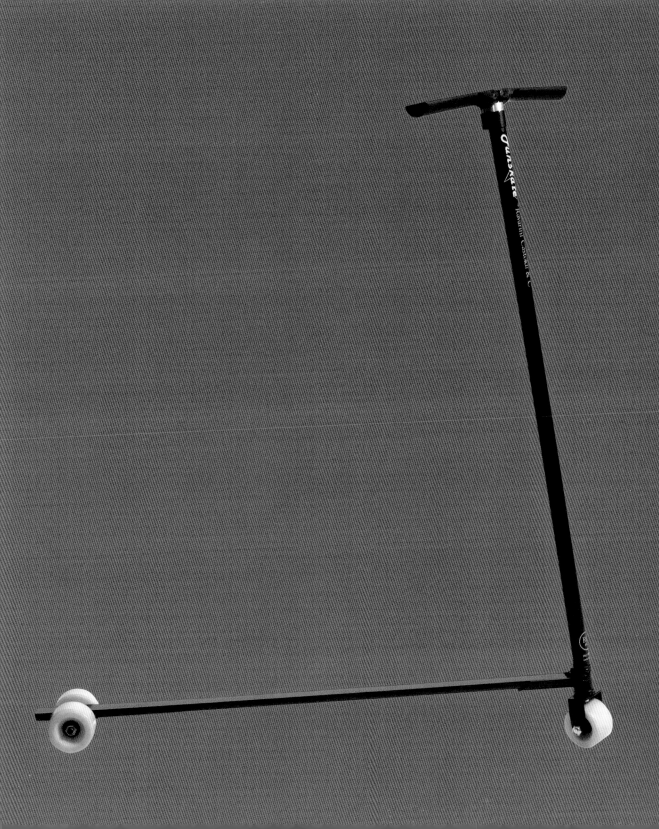

Teekanne	[**tay**kannuh]
tetera	[tay**tay**ra]
teiera	[tay**e**ra]
غلاية الشاي	[luh**lai**uht shai]
çaydanlık	[tshaidan**luhk**]
theepot	[**tay**pot]
teepôt	[**tay**pot]
きゅうす	[**kyoo**soo]
teapot	[**tee**pot]
théière	[tay**er**]

briquet	[bree**ke**]
Feuerzeug	[**foi**uhrtzoig]
mechero	[me**tsher**ro]
accendino	[atshen**dee**no]
قدّاحة	[khad**da**gha]
çakmak	[tshak**mak**]
aansteker	[**ahn**staykuhr]
oanstekker	[**ohn**stekkuhr]
ライター	[**rai**ta]
lighter	[**lai**tuh]

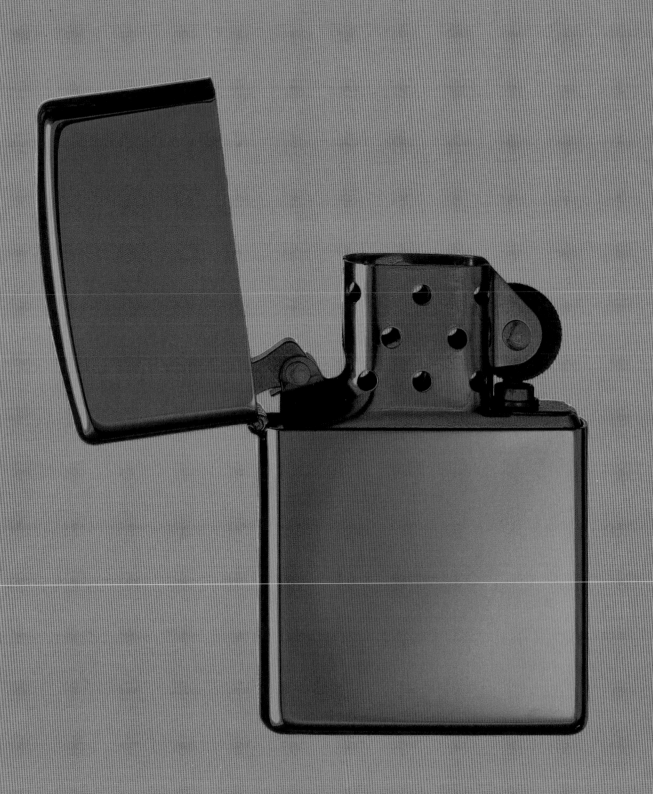

chain	[tshayn]
chaîne	[shenuh]
Kette	[kettuh]
cadena	[kadayna]
catena	[kattayna]
سلسلة	[seelseela]
zincir	[zeendzheer]
ketting	[ketting]
keatling	[ketling]
くさり	[koosaree]

ちょうぞう [tshohzoh]

sculpture [skulptyuh]

statue [stahtew]

Büste [bewstuh]

escultura [eskooltoora]

statua [statooa]

تمثال [teemthel]

heykel [heykel]

beeld [baylt]

boarstbyld [borstbeelt]

snorkel	[snurkl]
シュノーケル	[shnohkerroo]
snorkel	[snorkl]
tuba	[tewbah]
Schnorchel	[shnorghuhl]
tubo de respiración	[toobo day respeerathion]
respiratore	[respeeratoruh]
أنبوبة تنفس	[oonboobuht tennuhfoos]
şnorkel	[shnorkel]
snorkel	[snorkuhl]

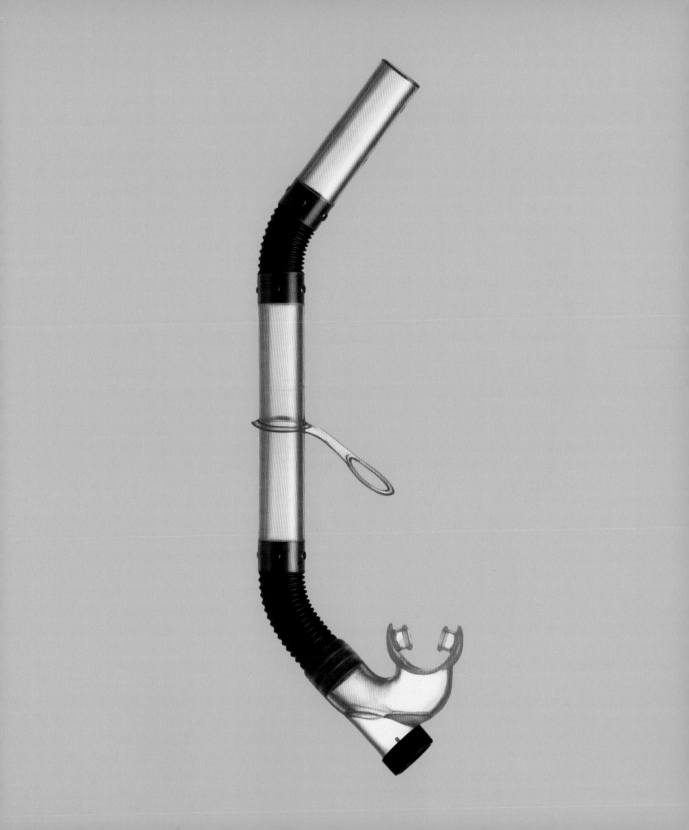

bord	[bort]
itensboard	[eetuhnsbo-aht]
さら	[sara]
plate	[playt]
assiette	[asyet]
Teller	[telluh]
plato	[platto]
piatto	[peeatto]
صحن	[seghn]
tabak	[tabak]

lamba	[lamba]
lamp	[lamp]
lampe	[lampuh]
ランプ	[rampoo]
lamp	[lemp]
lampe	[lamp]
Lampe	[lampuh]
lámpara	[lampara]
lampada	[lampada]
مصباح	[meesbagh]

سكين جيب   [see**keen** zhaib]

çakı   [tsha**kkuh**]

zakmes   [**zak**mes]

bûsmês   [**boos**mes]

ポケットナイフ   [**pok**ketnaifuh]

pocketknife   [**pokkuht**naif]

canif   [ka**neef**]

Taschenmesser   [**tash**uhnmessuhr]

navaja   [na**bagh**a]

temperino   [tempe**ree**no]

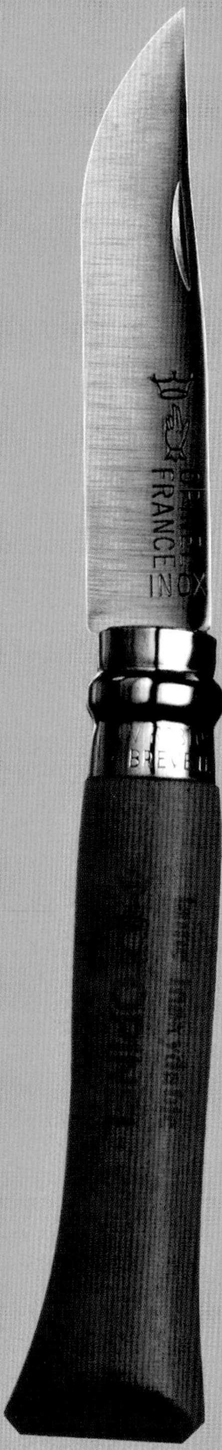
FRANCE
INOX

scodella	[sko**della**]
طنجرة	[**tan**zhara]
kâse	[kya**se**]
kom	[kom]
kom	[kom]
どんぶり	[**dom**boree]
bowl	[boal]
bol	[bol]
Schüssel	[**shew**suhl]
cuenco	[koo**en**koh]

termómetro	[termohmetro]
termometro	[termomaytro]
مقياس الحرارة	[meekyas al harrara]
termometre	[termometre]
thermometer	[termoamaytuh]
termometer	[termoamaytuh]
たいおんけい	[taionke]
thermometer	[thuhrmomuhtr]
thermomètre	[termoametr]
Thermometer	[termoamaytuhr]

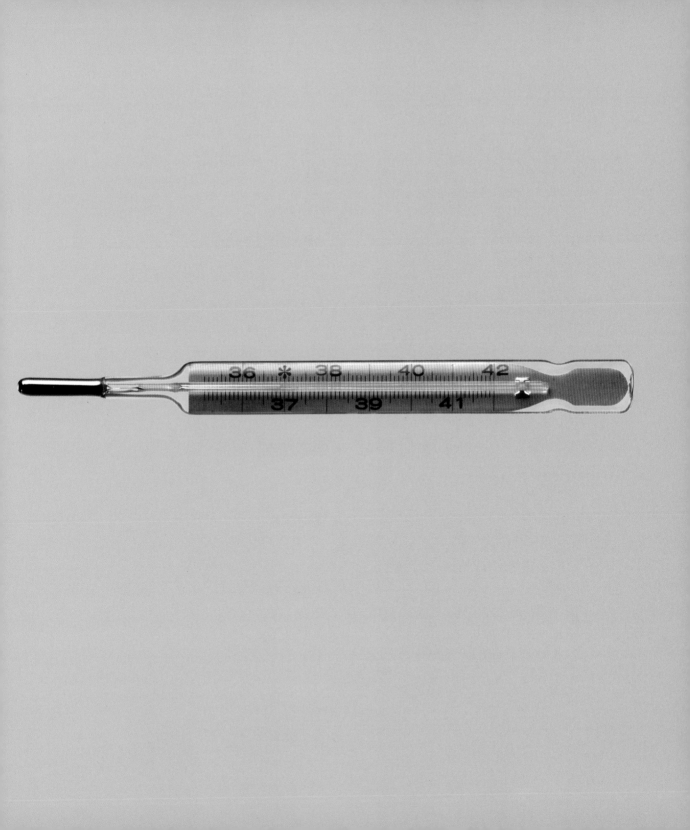

Schrank	[shrank]
armario	[armaryo]
cassettone	[kassettonuh]
خزانة	[khizehne]
dolap	[dolap]
kast	[kast]
kast	[kost]
たんす	[tansoo]
cupboard	[kubuhd]
armoire	[armooahr]

lampe de poche	[lamp duh **posh**]
Taschenlampe	[**tash**uhnlampuh]
linterna	[leen**ter**na]
lampadina tascabile	[lampa**dee**na tas**ka**beele]
لمبة جيب	[**lam**bat zhaib]
cep feneri	[**dzhep** fennerree]
zaklantaarn	[**zak**lantahruhn]
bûslantearne	[**boos**lantayrnuh]
ペンライト	[**pen**raito]
torch	[**tortsh**]

shoe	[shoo]
chaussure	[shoasewr]
Schuh	[shoo]
zapato	[zappato]
scarpa	[skarpa]
حذاء	[heedah-uh]
ayakkabı	[ayakkabbuh]
schoen	[sghoon]
skoech	[skoogh]
くつ	[kootsoo]

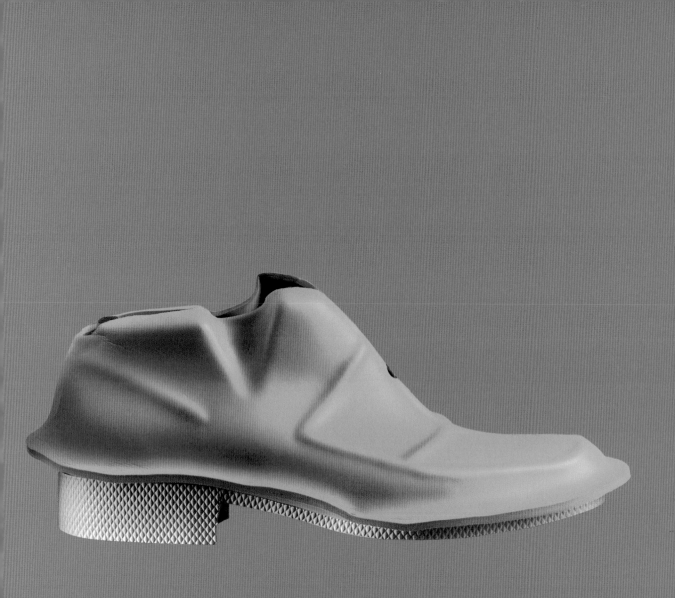

レモンのしぼり	[lemmuhnohsheeborree]
lemon squeezer	[lemuhn skweezuh]
presse-citron	[pres seetron]
Zitronenpresse	[tsitroanuhnpressuh]
exprimidor	[egspreemeedor]
spremilimoni	[zpraymeeleemonee]
عصارة	[assahra]
limon sıkacağı	[leemon suhkadzyahuh]
citruspers	[seetruhspers]
fruchtparse	[frughtparsuh]

tava	[tawa]
koekenpan	[kookuhpan]
koekepanne	[kookuhponnuh]
フライパン	[fraipan]
frying pan	[fraing pen]
poêle	[pooahl]
Pfanne	[Pfannuh]
sartén	[sartayn]
padella	[padella]
قدر كعك	[keedroo kahk]

stekker	[stekkuh]
プラグ	[prug]
plug	[plug]
fiche	[feesh]
Stecker	[shtekkuhr]
clavija	[klabigha]
spina elettrica	[speena aylettreeka]
قابس	[khuhbees]
fiş	[fyesh]
stekker	[stekkuh]

lepel	[laypuhl]
leppel	[lepl]
スプーン	[suhpoon]
spoon	[spoon]
cuillère	[kewyer]
Löffel	[lufl]
cuchara	[kootshara]
cucchiaio	[kookyayoh]
ملعقة	[meel-aka]
kaşık	[kashuhk]

tava   [tawa]

koekenpan   [kookuhpan]

koekepanne   [kookuhponnuh]

フライパン   [fraipan]

frying pan   [fraing pen]

poêle   [pooahl]

Pfanne   [Pfannuh]

sartén   [sartayn]

padella   [padella]

قدر كعك   [keedroo kahk]

كماشة   [kuhmehsha]

maşa   [massha]

tang   [tang]

tange   [tanguh]

ペンチ   [pentshee]

tongs   [tongs]

pince   [pins]

Zange   [tsanguh]

alicates   [alleekattays]

pinza   [peendza]

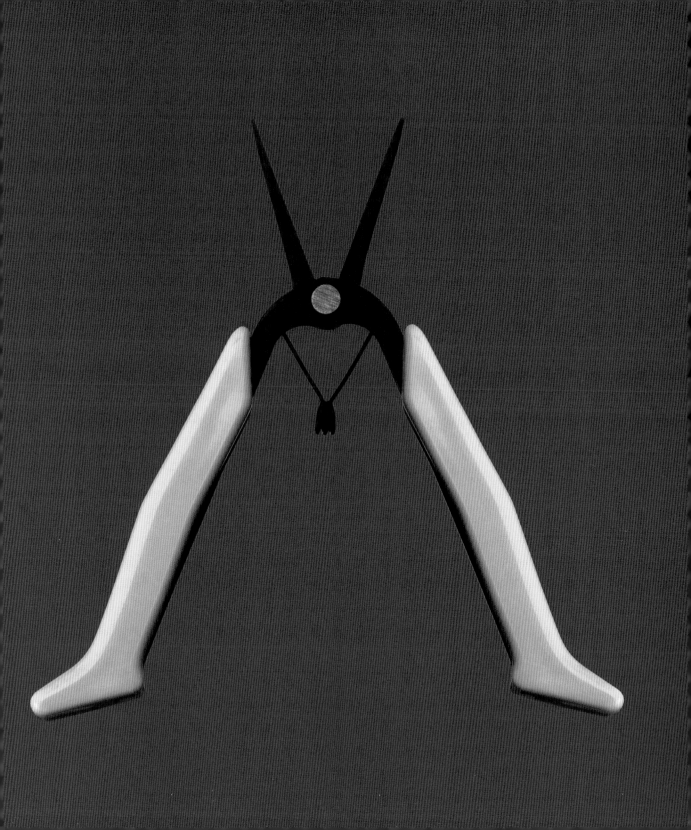

bottone	[bottonuh]
رن	[zir]
düğme	[dewhme]
knoop	[knoap]
knoop	[knoap]
ボタン	[botan]
button	[butuhn]
bouton	[booton]
Knopf	[knopf]
botón	[boaton]

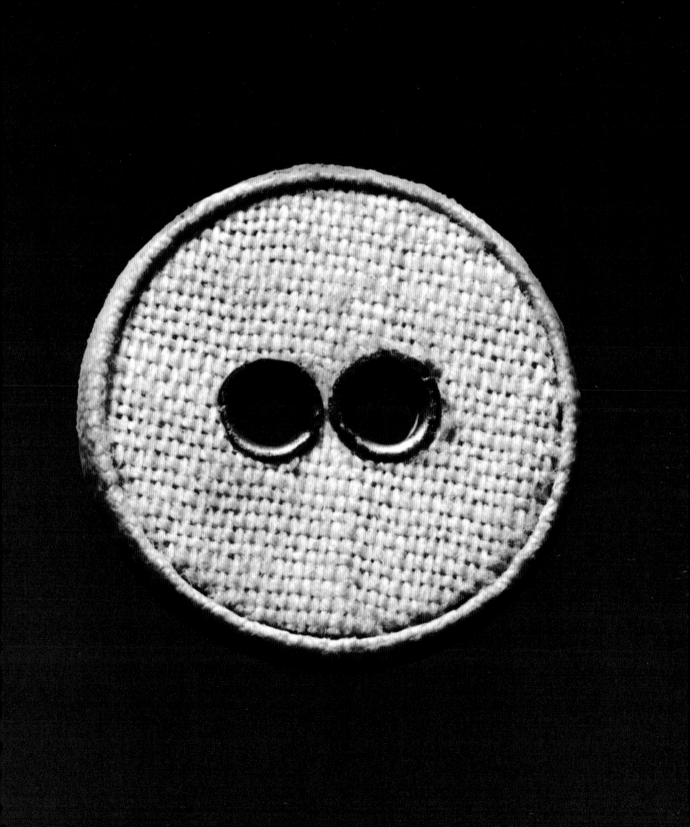

destornillador	[destorneelya**dor**]
cacciavite	[katsheeah**vee**tuh]
مفك	[mee**fuhk**]
tornavida	[torna**wee**da]
schroevendraaier	[**sroo**vuhdraiuhr]
skroevedraaier	[**skroo**vuhdraiuhr]
ねじまわし	[**ne**dzheema**wa**shee]
screwdriver	[**skroo**draivuh]
tournevis	[toorne**vees**]
Schraubenzieher	[**shrou**buhntseehuhr]

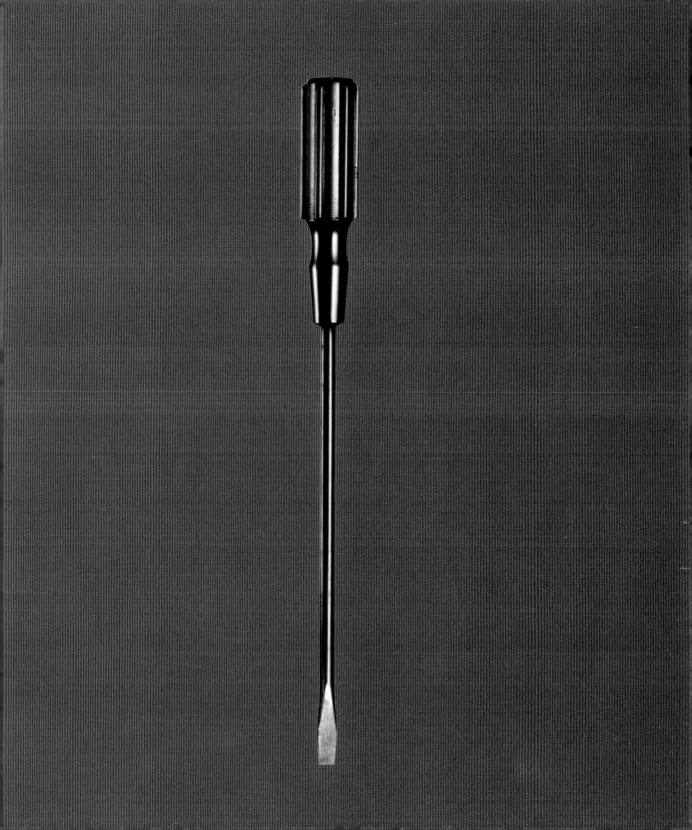

Computer	[kompyootuh]
ordenador	[ordaynador]
computer	[kompyootuh]
حاسوب	[hassoob]
bilgisayar	[beelgeesayar]
computer	[kompyootuh]
kompjûter	[kompyootuh]
コンピューター	[kompyoota]
computer	[kompyootuh]
ordinateur	[ordeenatuah]

passoire	[pasoo**ah**]
Sieb	[**zeep**]
escurridor	[eskooree**dor**]
colabrodo	[kola**bro**do]
مصفاة	[mees**faht**]
süzgeç	[sewz**getsh**]
vergiet	[ver**gheet**]
gatsjepanne	[**got**shuhponnuh]
ざる	[**za**roo]
colander	[**kol**luhnduh]

typewriter	[taipraituh]
machine à écrire	[masheen a aycreer]
Schreibmaschine	[shraipmasheenuh]
máquina de escribir	[mahkeena day skreebeer]
macchina da scrivere	[makkeena da skreevere]
آلة كاتبة	[ehluh kehteeba]
daktilo	[dakteelo]
typemachine	[teepmasheenuh]
typmasine	[teepmasheenuh]
タイプライター	[taipraita]

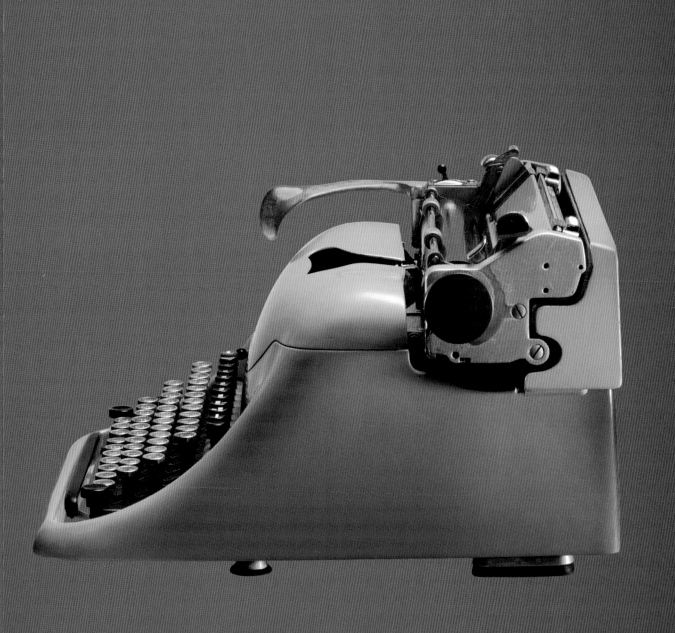

poatlead [po-ahtle-aht]

えんぴつ [empeetsoo]

pencil [pensuhl]

crayon [kreyon]

Bleistift [blaisteeft]

lápiz [lapeeth]

matita [mateeta]

قلم الرصاص [khuhlum arrasas]

kurşun kalem [koorshoon kalem]

potlood [potloat]

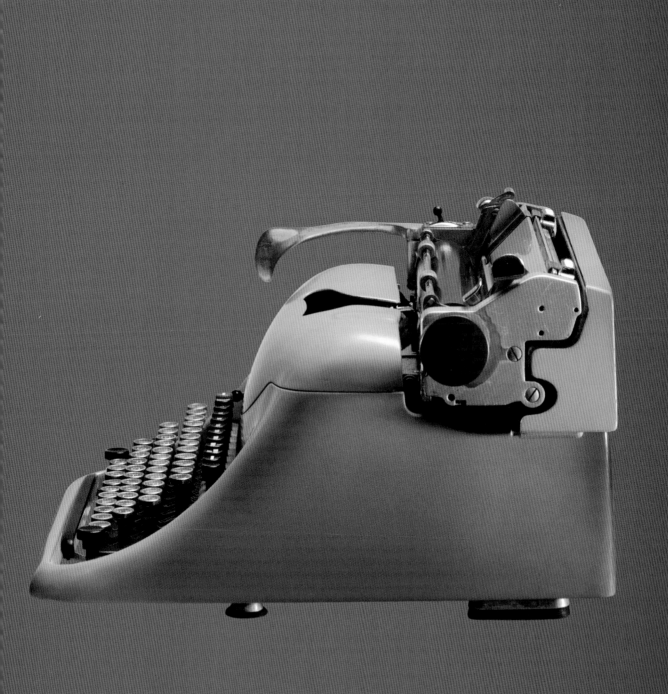

ラケット [rak**ket**to]

tennis racket [**ten**nuhs rekkuht]

raquette de tennis [ra**ket** de ten**nees**]

Tennisschläger [**ten**neesshlayguhr]

raqueta de tenis [ra**ket**ta day **ten**nees]

racchetta da tennis [rak**ket**ta da **ten**nees]

مضرب التنس [**mee**drab **ten**nees]

tenis raketi [**te**nnees rahkettee]

tennisracket [**ten**nuhsrekkuht]

tennisracket [**ten**nuhsrekkuht]

poatlead	[po-ahtle-aht]
えんぴつ	[empeetsoo]
pencil	[pensuhl]
crayon	[kreyon]
Bleistift	[blaisteeft]
lápiz	[lapeeth]
matita	[mateeta]
قلم الرصاص	[khuhlum arrasas]
kurşun kalem	[koorshoon kalem]
potlood	[potloat]

BRUYNZEEL HOLLAND | 1505 | TECHNITEK HIGH GRADE | 4 B

stopcontact   [stopkontakt]

stopkontakt   [stopkontakt]

コンセント   [konsento]

power point   [pouuh point]

prise   [prees]

Steckdose   [shtekdoasuh]

enchufe   [entshoofay]

presa di corrente   [praysa di korrente]

مقبس كهرباء   [meekbassoo kharabah-ee

priz   [preez]

jilet   [zheelet]

scheermes   [sghayrmes]

skearmês   [skayrmes]

かみそり   [kameesorree]

razor   [rayzuh]

rasoir   [raswah]

Rasiermesser   [rahseermessuhr]

maquinilla de afeitar   [makeeneelya day afaytar]

rasoio   [rasoyo]

موسى الحلاقة   [moosa al heelakha]

سكين [seekeen]

bıçak [buhtshak]

mes [mes]

mês [mes]

ナイフ [naifoo]

knife [naif]

couteau [kootoa]

Messer [messuhr]

cuchillo [kootsheelyo]

coltello [koltello]

telefono	[taylefono]
هاتف	[hehteef]
telefon	[telefon]
telefoon	[tayluhfoan]
tillefoan	[tilluhfo-ahn]
でんわ	[denwa]
telephone	[teluhfoan]
téléphone	[taylayfoan]
Telefon	[taylayfoan]
teléfono	[taylayfono]

cronómetro [kroa**noh**maytro]

cronometro [krono**no**maytro]

ساعة إيقاف [**se-**aht ee**khuhf**]

kronometre [krono**me**tre]

stopwatch [**stop**wotsh]

stopwatch [**stop**wotsh]

ストップウォッチ [stophu**wot**shee]

stopwatch [**stop**wotsh]

chronomètre [krono**metr**]

Stoppuhr [**shtop**oor]

ca 1955
Ko Verzuu
ADO (NL)
l 29,5 cm
hout, metaal, rubber /
wood, metal, rubber

Ato Mat 1957
Max Bill (CH)
Gebr. Junghans AG (D)
⌀ 30,4 cm
metaal, glas /
metal, glass

Feuerbach 1942
H. Bodmer
Leipzig (D)
h 33,7 cm
papier, linnen /
paper, linnen

1989
Philippe Starck
Fluocaril (F)
l 19,5 cm
kunststof / plastic

Randstad ruler 1991
N | P | K (NL)
l 35 cm
kunststof, rubber /
plastic, rubber

Sports Walkman 1982-1983
Sony design team
Sony Corporation (J)
h 10 cm
kunststof / plastic

Alhambra ca 1920
Jac. Jongert
NV United Glassworks (NL)
h 26 cm
glas / glass

ca 1875
Christopher Dresser
Coalbrookdale Co. (GB)
h 1,85 m
gietijzer / cast iron

1956
Rob Parry, Emil Truyen
PTT (NL)
h 53 cm
kunststof / plastic

Ovata, KO 1365 1928
H.P. Berlage
Glasfabriek 'Leerdam' (NL)
h 15 cm
kristal / crystal

ca 1985
EMI Associates
Silky Gomtaro UM (J)
l 42,7 cm
metaal, kunststof /
metal, plastic

prototype 1979
Michele De Lucchi
Rabbolini, Memphis (I)
h 20 cm
hout, kunststof /
wood, plastic

ca 1996
Muji (J)
h 9 cm
aluminium / aluminium

ca 1880-1900
anoniem / anonymous (NL)
l 13 cm
ijzer, glas / iron, glass

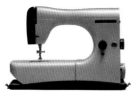

Lydia 1955
Marcello Nizzoli
Necchi S.p.A. (I)
h 29 cm
metaal / metal

ca 1950-1960
NEN-KIWA (NL)
l 11 cm
metaal / metal

T 1000 1963
Rieter Rams
Braun AG (D)
h 25 cm
aluminium, leer /
aluminium, leather

Leica 1A 1914-1936 (1930)
Oskar Barnack
Ernst Leitz AG (D)
l 13,3 cm
metaal, glas /
metal, glass

Mach 2000 1975
Roger Tallon
Lip (F)
l 24 cm
rubber, metaal, glas /
rubber, metal, glass

Edding 1700 ca 1980
Edding (D)
l 14 cm
kunststof / plastic

1943
Bruno Mathson
fa. Karl Mathson (s)
h 63,5 cm
hout, metaal / wood, metal

Armand Roulin 1888
Vincent van Gogh (NL/F)
h 91 cm
olieverf op linnen, hout /
oil on linnen, wood

ca 1910
Philips Gloeilampenfabriek
(NL)
h 10,5 cm
glas, metaal / glass, metal

ca 1945
Andries Copier
Glasfabriek 'Leerdam' (NL)
h 20 cm
glas / glass

Ballbarrow 1974
James Dyson
Hozelock-ASL (GB)
h 62,5 cm
kunststof, metaal /
plastic, metal

Blouson Bridgestone 1985
Giorgio Giugiaro
Bridgestone Cycle Co. Ltd.
(J)
h 100 cm
staal, rubber / steel, rubber

ca 1930-1940
Plumb (GB)
l 15 cm
hout, kunststof /
wood, plastic

Abacus II 1980
Martin Riddiford, Frazer
design
Brinloc (GB)
h 11,3 cm
kunststof / plastic

W&LT interactive 2,
Summercollection 1996
1996
Walter van Beirendonck
h 12,5 cm
kunststof / plastic

ca 1980
anoniem / anonymous (J)
l 9,6 cm
hout / wood

1899 (1997)
J. Vaaler (N)
l 5,3 cm
metaal / metal

Two hands 1995
Konstantin Grcic
Authentics (D)
Ø 59 cm
kunststof / plastic

1951-1952
Charles Eames, Ray Eames
Herman Miller (USA)
h 62,5 cm
kunststof, metaal /
plastic, metal

Robe doublure 1996
Martin Margiela (B)
Staff (I)
maat 38 / size 42
zeefdruk op textiel /
silkscreen on textile

ca 1930-1940
Philips (NL)
l 19 cm
metaal, bakeliet

1995
Ruud Jan Kokke (NL)
Becker KG (D)
l 94 cm
hout, rubber /
wood, rubber

Neto 1954
Antonia Campi
Ermenegildo Collini (I)
l 25,4 cm
staal / steel

1650-1700
(NL)
h 77 cm
hout / wood

Capella 1975
Gertrud Vasegaard
Den kgl. Porcelainsfabrik
(DK)
h 6,5 cm
porselein / porcelain

1957
Arne Jakobsen
A. Michelsen (DK)
l 21 cm
roestvrij staal /
stainless steel

Standard ware ca 1950
Leach Pottery (GB)
h 25 cm
steengoed / stoneware

Funscate 1985
Ravarini Castoldi
Ravarini Castoldi & Co. (I)
h 100 cm
metaal, kunststof /
metal, plastic

Mask I 1976
Ralph Osterhout
Tekna (USA)
h 8,7 cm
kunststof / plastic

ca 1970
Lucie Rie (GB)
h 22 cm
steengoed / stoneware

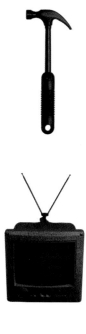

Kuroht 1985
Daik (J)
l 27,7 cm
metaal, rubber /
metal, rubber

Zippo 1932 (1997)
George Grant Blaisdell
Zippo Manufacturing
Company (USA)
h 5,6 cm
metaal / metal

Jim Nature 1993
Philippe Starck
SABA GMBH (D)
h 37 cm
kunststof, hout /
plastic, wood

1500-1600
(NL)
l 12,5 cm
brons / bronze

Othorhinologische kop van Venus / Othorhinological head of Venus 1964
Salvador Dali (E)
h 71 cm
gips / plaster

ca 1890
Joseph Opinel
Opinel S.A. (F)
l 19,5 cm
hout, roestvrij staal / wood, stainless steel

1987
Ralph Osterhout
Tekna (USA)
l 41,3 cm
kunststof / plastic

ca 1951
Hans Coper, Lucie Rie (GB)
h 7 cm
steengoed / stoneware

1903-1904
Henry van de Velde (B)
Königliche Sächsische Porzelanmanufactur, Meissen (D)
⌀ 23,2 cm
porselein / porcelain

ca 1950-1960
Sturm (D)
l 19 cm
glas, metaal / glass, metal

PH 1 1925
Poul Henningsen
Deutsche PH-Lampen-gesellschaft MBH (D)
h 43 cm
glas, metaal / glass, metal

1600-1700
(NL)
h 2,25 m
hout / wood

Mag light ca 1980-1990
Mag instrument (USA)
l 31,5 cm
metaal, glas / metal, glass

1500-1600
(NL)
l 13,5 cm
hout / wood

prototype *Foam fashion*
1996
Liselotte Bekkers (NL)
l 32,5 cm
EVA foam / EVA foam

Tefal bis 1956
F. Gregoir
Tefal (F)
l 45,5 cm
metaal, kunststof /
metal, plastic

ca 1930
anoniem / anonymous (GB)
h 10 cm
kunststof/ plastic

ca 1985
anoniem / anonymous
(J)
h 15 cm
kunststof, metaal /
plastic, metal

ca 1930
anoniem / anonymous
h 7,5 cm
kunststof, metaal /
plastic, metal

ca 1950-1975
anoniem / anonymous
⌀ 1,3 cm
metaal, textiel /
metal, textile

ca 1989
anoniem / anonymous
l 38 cm
metaal / metal

Challange nr. 1 ca 1975
Slazenger (GB)
l 69 cm
hout, leer / wood, leather

M 20 1981
Ettore Sottsass jr.,
Antonio Macchi Cassia,
George Sowden
Olivetti S.p.A. (I)
h 46,5 cm
kunststof, metaal /
plastic, metal

ca 1958
Piet Zwart
Bruynzeels Potloden-
fabriek (NL)
l 17,5 cm
hout, grafiet / wood, graphite

1898
CV Petrus Regout & Co.
(NL)
⌀ 17,3 cm
aardewerk / earthenware

1900-1930
anoniem / anonymous (D)
⌀ 5,8 cm
porselein, metaal /
porcelain, metal

Lexicon 80 1948
Marcello Nizzoli
Olivetti S.p.A. (I)
h 23,8 cm
metaal / metal

GBS, reg. no. 809050
ca 1930
anoniem / anonymous
h 8 cm
kunststof / plastic

1848
John Bell
Joseph Rodgers & Sons /
Summeleys Art
Manufactures (GB)
l 33,5 cm
ivoor, metaal / ivory, metal

1931
Jean Heiberg (N)
Siemens Ltd. (GB)
h 14 cm
bakeliet / bakelite

1970-1975
Heuer-Leonidas SA (CH)
⌀ 5,2 cm
metaal, glas / metal, glass

The pronunciation

The pronunciation of the words is written in English.

Things: collection Boijmans Van Beuningen Museum

© 1998, Boijmans Van Beuningen Museum Rotterdam

Concept, editing
Thimo te Duits

Research
Margreet Eijkelenboom-Vermeer
Marcel Brouwer

Translation
NOB Translation Dept., Hilversum

Design
Gracia Lebbink, Amsterdam

Typesetting
Holger Schoorl

Photography
Gerrit Schreurs, Rijswijk
ass. Pieter Leenheer

Image manipulation
Mischa van Ginneken
Jacqueline van den Boom
Gerrit Schreurs Fotografie, Rijswijk

Printing
Snoeck-Ducaju & Zoon, Gent (B)

Assistance
J.J. van Cappellen

ISBN
90-6918-188-6

Sponsors:

Corporate Members of
the Boijmans Van Beuningen Museum

ABN AMRO Bank N.V.; CALDIC; Internatio-Müller NV;
DURA BOUW ROTTERDAM B.V.; Aon Hudig;
Koninklijke Nedlloyd N.V.; Unilever; Loyens & Volkmaars;
Koninklijke Econosto N.V.; Koninklijke Pakhoed N.V.;
MeesPierson N.V.; Gimbrère en Dohmen Software B.V.;
Hollandsche Beton Maatschappij bv; Generale Bank
Nederland N.V.; Moret Ernst & Young; Nauta Dutilh;
Siemens Nederland N.V.; PTT Telecom District
Rotterdam; Bakker Beheer Barendrecht BV; Mobil Oil B.V.;
Nationale Nederlanden ; Van der Vorm Vastgoed B.V.;
Heineken Nederland B.V.; Glaxo Wellcome B.V.;
HAL Investments B.V.; KPMG Accountants Belasting-
adviseurs Consultants ; EOE-Optiebeurs; SGS Nederland
B.V.; Stichting Organisatie van Effectenhandelaren te
Rotterdam; Hagé International B.V.; Parc Makelaars;
Nidera Handelscompagnie b.v.; Automobielbedrijf
J. van Dijk & Dochters b.v.; KOEN VISSER GROEP;
Stad Rotterdam Verzekeringen; Gebrs. Coster Beheer B.V.;
Croon Elektrotechniek B.V.; Van Dijk Delft B.V.; Dionijs
Burger Groep B.V.; Europees Massagoed- Overslagbedrijf
(EMO) bv; Blauwhoed bv; Gemeente Rotterdam, Afdeling
Externe Betrekkingen

Erasmus Stichting   Mondriaan Stichting   Museum Boijmans Van Beuningen Rotterdam